★★★★★
Fantastic satire
This explores some topics often unexplored and does so with some great witty satire. Well done
— Alexa

★★★★★
Five Stars
Original, wise, and well written.
— Joshua Hirsch

★★★★★
Hauntingly beautiful and profound.
Beautifully written and emotionally stirring. Your soul will be wrestling with this book long after you've finished reading it. Part Rumi, part Khalil Gibran, and part William Blake, yet totally unique and authentic and unexpected.
— Jonathan B.

OUTLOOK PABULUM

STEVEN GOMES JR.

Outlook Pabulum
Copyright © 2021 by Steven Gomes Jr.

All rights reserved. No part of this publication may be reproduced, distributed, or transmitted in any form or by any means, including photocopying, recording, or other electronic or mechanical methods, without the prior written permission of the author, except in the case of brief quotations embodied in critical reviews and certain other non-commercial uses permitted by copyright law.

ISBN
978-1-954932-38-8 (Paperback)
978-1-954932-37-1 (eBook)

OUTLOOK PABULUM

NOURISHMENT FOR THE MIND; SUSTENANCE; FOOD

To my Nana – Grace Stocks, who brought my mother into existence and shared her life experiences with me. She was the most open- minded person I have ever known.

To my Mother – Sylvia Stocks, who brought me into existence and taught me how to care, love, help others and give selflessly. Costs and fees would normally follow some of the things that she has done absolutely free of charge. She also told me that the dumbest question was a question not asked.

To my Father – Steven Gomez Sr, who taught me how to dream big, stand by what I believe in and, most importantly, dream big.

To my Brother – Marcus Garvey Gomes, the first person I loved more than myself, preparing me for fatherhood.

To my Son – Steven Gomes III, who will be an honorable man one day with all of my strengths and none of my weaknesses, and all of my hopes and none of my regrets.

To my High School Teacher – Mrs. Sarah Kosarko Williams, who convinced me to try this thing called "writing".

To my Friend – Daniel, who taught me the true meaning of research. He also taught me the importance of intellectual salvation.

To the Mother of my son – Stephanie Cave, who sat on my shoulder like an Angel not too long ago, telling me that I could take my scattered papers, bind them together and slowly change the World.

Thank you,

"Beauty isn't what you see in the mirror, it's who you see".

— **Jade A. Rivera**

Recipe

For years I have yearned to speak to the masses without talking. My mother told me that even as a child, I was a watcher, a thinker and very inquisitive. As a teen, my attributes intensified, together with a feeling of extreme loneliness. I was quickly learning there was a backlash to asking questions. I learned about opposition, making your own path, and peer pressure.

As I got older I found that these childhood experiences weren't confined to being a child at all. I always dared to be different and live outside the box of normality. Enlightenment has always been my destination. It troubled me deeply that my path was considered rebellious by some family and friends. It took me years to get comfortable with my position. If I questioned the pastor at my local church, I was questioning God and would shortly sit at the Devil's right hand for wanting clarity. The Bible states: "Seek and you shall find". I also learned that others profited from me being ignorant (ignoring what is clearly in front of me.)

I have always felt that on many occasions our educational system helps us as well as our children to bypass research, which is one of the most crucial steps in learning. This is how we accept the "edited" dictation called education as fact before we can prove anything. Giving a child an excellent grade for memorization and not thinking may have contributed over the years to the masses of people acting on what they are told and not what they have found. Plagued by the desire to know why we indulge in practices that are disastrous to our wellbeing, questions burn in my being. Questions like, What is the difference between the brain and the mind? What is the difference between fantasy and reality? Is a belief or the truth worth living for? What's my purpose? How do I affect the financial statement of the Tycoon that possibly runs my life? Are all of our differences in many ways relative? Can choices, time and forgiveness be the sum of the human experience? I guess the calamity occurs when we stop asking.

Common sense can be the bricks that repave burned bridges. Pabulum will feed our wits and expand our capabilities. Children from all backgrounds play together in the sand until Adults ruin everything. Simplicity is life. We come into this world naked, innocent and full of life. Hanging on to these qualities throughout life would seem like a better goal to shoot for than the most coveted destination in heaven. If we can ever make sense of ourselves, we would truly understand the World. Pain presents itself often to those who have lost their fight.

I wonder, after all of the mind-conditioning, emotional pain, broken promises, depression and let-downs, do you still dare to dream? Can you travel through different ideas and arrive at a conscious destination? Can you trust me for just a couple of pages? I hope to anger you, challenge you, inspire you, and open your natural imagination separate from fantasy. I hope I can help you remember rather than teach you. Remember your emotions before, in a lot of ways, technology took them from you. Remember your true love before lust. Remember that we get second chances all the time, called "tomorrow".

Let's aspire to perfection, the way our elders intended us to be. Let us keep with us the notion that there is no harmony in war. I hope to give you love and inspiration through my words. Regardless of race, color or creed, I only have the best of intentions for all who have the best of intentions in their heart for me and my family. Let us care about humanity and our place in it. Let us give more than we take. Please remember my words and know that I have given them to you from the purest place in my heart.

Be well, be more than what we desire to physically attain. Be more than what you look like, be more than your social circle. Be more than those lengthy glances in the mirror or anything else that casts a reflection, for you were beautiful in your mother's womb. I've always felt like a servant of humanity, so it shouldn't come as any surprise that I will be your server today or any other day you choose to let Pabulum feed your inner Fat Owl.

Slosh

It takes approximately four hours for the human body to digest food. How long does it take to mentally and emotionally digest Pabulum? My Pabulum is marinated and seasoned with care, positivity and respect. My Pabulum can be compared to vegetables. Vegetables don't always taste good but are necessary for a strong body as negative forces propel sticks and stones your way. My Pabulum will also strengthen your trust in your eyesight, making you believe what you see and not see only what you believe. My Pabulum will make ignorance obsolete. The price on my menu is patience and your willingness to temporarily step outside all comfort zones in order to think outside the box (T.O.T.B). My only request is that the reader chews his/her Pabulum carefully.

Menu
Caloric Intake

Recipe vi
Slosh ix

Daydreaming

Dig	740 Cal	 2
Eavesdropper	610 Cal	 3
Ascendency	790 Cal	 4
Iffy	370 Cal	 5
The Unbroken	440 Cal	 6
Broken	490 Cal	 7
Fracas	505 Cal	 8
My Detriment	471 Cal	 9
Will	388 Cal	 11
Disbelief	492 Cal	 12
From A Distance	683 Cal	 13
Hearsay	449 Cal	 14
Thankless	612 Cal	 15
Loser's Limp	437 Cal	 16
Awakening	581 Cal.	 18
Her over We	403 Cal	 19

Angels	507 Cal	20
Treason	367 Cal	21
Observe	519 Cal	22
Khem	565 Cal	23
Sounds of Deception	603 Cal	24
Overstood	373 Cal	25
Destitute of Light	409 Cal	26
Win For Losing	511 Cal	27
Becoming	336 Cal	28

Daydreaming Pabulum

Pabulum 1	2182 Cal	30
Pabulum 2	2182 Cal	31
Pabulum 3	2182 Cal	32
Pabulum 4	2182 Cal	33
Pabulum 5	2182 Cal	34
Pabulum 6	2182 Cal	35
Pabulum 7	2182 Cal	36
Pabulum 8	2182 Cal	37
Pabulum 9	2182 Cal	38
Pabulum 10	2182 Cal	39
Pabulum 11	2182 Cal	40
Pabulum 12	2182 Cal	41
Pabulum 13	2182 Cal	42
Daydreaming's Why...	1232 Cal	43

Reality

Realization	200 Cal	47
Emotions	140 Cal	48
Apathy	170 Cal	49
Enlightenment	130 Cal	50
Last Cry	100 Cal	51
The Unknower	270 Cal	52
Pressure	40 Cal	53
The Chase	98 Cal	54
Velvet	127 Cal	55
Pang	69 Cal	56
The Gimmies	102 Cal	57
The Twist	181 Cal	58
Asylum	156 Cal	59
What a Web We Weave	142 Cal	60
The Vanishing	84 Cal	62
Callow	93 Cal	63
Four Legs	148 Cal	64
Fortune	76 Cal	65

Reality's Pabulum

Pabulum 14	300 Cal	67
Pabulum 15	300 Cal	68
Pabulum 16	300 Cal	69
Pabulum 17	300 Cal	70
Pabulum 18	300 Cal	71
Pabulum 19	300 Cal	72
Pabulum 20	300 Cal	73
Pabulum 21	300 Cal	74
Pabulum 22	300 Cal	75
Pabulum 23	300 Cal	76
Reality's Why	482 Cal	77

War

No Pardon	435 Cal	81
Putrid	419 Cal	82
War Posture	491 Cal	84
Hero	562 Cal	85
Five Stars	420 Cal	86
Exceed	600 Cal	88
Charge	409 Cal	89
The Switch	516 Cal	90

War's Pabulum

Pabulum 24	720 Cal	92
Pabulum 25	720 Cal	93
Pabulum 26	720 Cal	94
Pabulum 27	720 Cal	95
Pabulum 28	720 Cal	96
Pabulum 29	720 Cal	97
Pabulum 30	720 Cal	98
Pabulum 31	720 Cal	99
War's Why	378 Cal	100

Love

SG3	2690 Cal	104
Fool's Gold	2090 Cal	105
Tickled	2060 Cal	106
Inspiration	2290 Cal	107
Daze	2590 Cal	108
Frenzy	2020 Cal	109
Impulse	2780 Cal	110
Resistance	1760 Cal	111
Untouchable	1890 Cal	112
Sunset	1920 Cal	113
Southeast	2560 Cal	114

Loathe	2010 Cal	115
The Veil	2180 Cal	116
Fancy	2480 Cal	117
The Battery, the Rose and the Rain	300 Cal	118

Love's Pabulum

Pabulum 32	1828 Cal	120
Pabulum 33	1828 Cal	121
Pabulum 34	1828 Cal	122
Pabulum 35	1828 Cal	123
Pabulum 36	1828 Cal	124
Pabulum 37	1828 Cal	125
Pabulum 38	1828 Cal	126
Pabulum 39	1828 Cal	127
Pabulum 40	1828 Cal	128
Pabulum 41	1828 Cal	129
Pabulum 42	1828 Cal	130
Pabulum 43	1828 Cal	131
Pabulum 44	1828 Cal	132
Pabulum 45	1828 Cal	133
Love's Why	2987 Cal	134

Pray

Petition	490 Cal	138
Prayer 1	880 Cal	139
Prayer 2	880 Cal	140
Prayer 3	880 Cal	141

Prayer's Pabulum

Pabulum 46	1522 Cal.	143
Pabulum 47	1522 Cal.	144
Pabulum 48	1522 Cal.	145
Pabulum 49	1522 Cal.	146
Pabulum 50	1522 Cal.	147
Pabulum 51	1522 Cal.	148
Pabulum 52	1522 Cal.	149
Pabulum 53	1522 Cal.	150
Pabulum 54	1522 Cal.	151
Pabulum 55	1522 Cal.	152
Pabulum 56	1522 Cal.	153
Pabulum 57	1522 Cal.	154
Pabulum 58	1522 Cal.	155
Pabulum 59	1522 Cal.	156
Prayers Why	1979 Cal	158

The Binge

Keepsake	4281 Cal	162
What it seems	2622 Cal	167
The Loudest Whisper	3347 Cal	169
True Story	1937 Cal	171
The Weak Eat The Weak	3168 Cal	173
Goddess	1718 Cal	175
The Vision	2229 Cal	178
Reflection	1677 Cal	181
The Binge…Why?	3173 Cal	183
Do you like Riddles?	38 Cal	184
Cessation	4 Cal	193

I open my ears so I can see
I see stars in the water
My head is in the clouds
The clouds are on my shoulders
Who needs to run when you can fly?

I'm sorry, you will have to excuse me, sometimes I catch myself…

Daydreaming

Dig

Who colors the rainbow? What if the seasons act as four different perspectives of the year? What if a butterfly was most beautiful as a caterpillar? If the Earth constantly rotates, does humanity stand still? If good needs bad and beauty needs ugly, maybe we're simply forced to pick a side. If the Sun gives us life from sunrays sent years ago, can we say we truly live in the past? Is life so challenging that we blink so we only have to view the World for seconds at a time? Is freedom a funny little word created by captors? If humanity were free, would there be a word to describe it? And if I were God, would I tell you when I was going to judge you or would I judge you through your children's eyes, when you least expect it? Who does, What if, How come, and if so, Why?

Eavesdropper

The birds have no stopping in them, effortless it seems. Constant motion in the skies that goes unnoticed…**at times, I envy**.
The best of both worlds, I believe.
To oversee our lives from above…**sometimes, I wish**. Taking the higher road, the road admired by the fallen. And their backs greet the sun…on their feet they walk, Only to tease humanity.
Shortly after, the sky summons its messengers.

Ascendency

Like a child would a piece of birthday cake
I grabbed a handful of fluffy cloud
To my dismay I came up with air
Seeming to have nothing I cried
Taking for granted my attempt, an owl with
a golden crown flew alongside me and said,
"Take it easy on yourself, son,
look at how far you've come.
All the success in the world won't make you a number.
Some of the things I see up here are unbelievable.
That horrific number 1 is the culprit."
"Who put so much status and self-worth
into the number 1?" I asked.
The owl smiled and said, "Whoever was number 2".
And in a blink of an eye, my little friend was gone.

Iffy

I'm wearing cement shoes in the ocean. The one with nothing usually can gain everything. The one with everything gains nothing. The fear of failure haunts me. The fear of success reminds me of my fear of failure again. My fear of flying reminds me of my fear of falling. It's sad to see someone meet their future and see only their past. I think they shot for the sky and forgot the stars were their goal. Can success be measured with a scale, ruler or bank account? Does any fear overshadow the other? No matter how uncertain, good or bad your fate may be, it probably has already chosen you.

The Unbroken

The truth is that a lie is. We yell with our mouths, muffle our actions, then wonder where change has gone. If we walk the same path every day, it is hardly a coincidence that we step in the very same spot once or twice. Does existence ever fade? Insanity seems to systematically pick its host. I remain anonymous. Isn't it insane to have a billion imaginary friends? We all stand in the center of our own world. We see only through our eyes. It's evident that we exist, but do they? I find my answer as I sleep in darkness and travel. I crack a smile as I sleep. I've lost track of time and space. It seems we have been given an opportunity at the possibility… and this remains unbroken.

Broken

Imagine a storm that never stopped, a relentless onslaught of rain and wind. The storm had no mercy. Sacred belongings were lost and never found. People just stopped looking, stopped caring…but how? The wind blew away memories and dreams. Wherever the people were, the wind brought them and kept them. Cyclonic winds reached unbelievable speeds, stirring jealously, deceit, self-hate, and depression. There seemed to be no end in sight. There are people now, it seems, that don't see the rain, don't feel the wind… numb to destruction. After a while the storm became normality. Generations even started to love the storm. They soon resented memories and belongings of the past. The wind was oppression; the rain was lies and the storm…that's where **invaders hide.** There was nowhere to run.

Fracas

You love, I respect
You compete, I challenge
You consume, I eat
You wish, I plan
You believe, I know
You stop, I refrain
You walk, I step
You grin, I laugh
You offer, I give
You hear, I listen
You touch, I feel
You teach, I enlighten
You discover, I find
You ignore, I tune out
You live on the brink, I live on the edge
You tell jokes, I tell riddles
You surround, I engulf
You feed hunger, I feed famine
You predict, I prophesize
You aspire for heaven; I aspire to go to other dimensions
You aim at the clouds; I aim for the stars.
Which are you?

My Detriment

Something has taken the smell of roses from me. What has turned anger inwards? Where I would've, should've gone forces me to ponder what I should've, could've done. To hold purity at this moment seems undeserving, a solution just waiting for the problem to manifest. I wait, unsatisfied thus far with my results. Annoyed are those who attempt to waste monetary hope on futility. Words have left me. I can only gesture. I must return to a place I've never been before, sifting through dirt to come out clean. I beg time for patience, playing in the truth when I should be drinking from it, thought of as a coward when I hide within myself. I smile to myself. I'm careful not to show too many teeth. I regroup, face east and wait 24 hours to see as a child does for the first time. Drowning in procrastination, sometimes hoping time doesn't notice me and start ticking again. Suppressing my purpose for money…if only I had learned sooner what I was never taught, colonization of options. I get the blame for not choosing, afraid of the creation and not the creator. In the heat of it all, the pressure, the hope, the dreams, the wants, the needs, the regrets, the I'm-sorrys, the I-hate-yous, the I-love-yous, the please-please-pleases, the wait-just-a-second and all that jazz…the seasons still change, rain falls certain of its destination at my feet. The sun seems to rise and set but is always present even when our backs are turned. I've often taken the road of the meantime in between time. Indulging in things that will kill me slower, giving me time to figure these things out. Why not? In the end I will stand. I will win the game, knowing the game I play is for survival not fun. Those who couldn't see will, those who couldn't hear want to. More than anyone I want peace of mind. I need closure, my wounds need to heal. I need to smell those roses again…Don't we all?

Will

Suddenly the deepest silence surrounds me. Beams of light approach me. A face starts to form. The face tells me that it will give me the key that will unlock the door that holds my purpose hostage. However, it is never mentioned that there are millions of keys on the floor. The lights go out! Feeling deceived, I yell, "What's going on?" Feeling along the ground I touch something that feels like a hand. Paralyzed with fear I discontinue my pursuit. Faint sounds in the distance are becoming clearer and sound like voices. I am also starting to hear heavy breathing and crying. Common sense tells me that if there are one million keys on the floor, then there must be an equal number of participants, at least. Will anyone ever find their purpose. I wonder if we are sifting through mountains of keys in search of the same door.

Disbelief

Misery welcomes selfishness.
I indulge from time to time.
Each day reinforcing my reality.
Each morning shining light on my
choices and mistakes.
The arrogance of youth is humbled
as time patiently waits.
Dangling from a cliff.
All of my strength is given to the weak.
I find my energy drained, unable
to pull myself up.
I look up for my caped savior and find no one.
Where is my rescuer when I'm in need?
Where are the uplifting words I most
generously gave away?
Who saves a Hero?

From A Distance

It's hard to see what others don't, hard to care when others won't. A man walks his own path. The truth is hidden and no one dares look. A world where the message is lost and the messenger is slain. The end is certain, but is it near? A world minus hypocrisy, plus community is simple math. Who saves the man with no home? Chasing happiness is temporary. My destination is somewhere deep in the valley, just above those mountains. I hear my breath and feel my heart. Even keel and in tune with my opposition. Dreaming I can handle, it's the nightmare I worry about. Being remembered as the King who stepped past his throne to sit on the floor haunts me. When the masses eat, drink, breathe green, finely woven cotton, it ignites a sort of hypnotic reality, making reality negotiable. Clouds seem to encase nature's mystery. They have the task of covering what lies ahead. They test our perceptional limitations. Time sedates us with chances. I'm never surprised at what I uncover.

Hearsay

I've heard of a place where birds sing constantly and babies chuckle with innocence. The first warm breeze after winter begins every day. Rain is always accompanied by the sun as those shiny little droplets tickle the hands and feet of humanity. I've heard of a place where words only bring smiles and cheer. War is unknown; every fruit is in arm's reach and as sweet as a first kiss. I've heard that the love there nurtures people's bodies. Poverty, starvation and greed are unknown words. Your level of respect for humanity governs your social status. Each step is along the beach where soulmates are only one glance away. All debts are paid and tender is issued with hugs. I've only heard of such a place.

Thankless

Ashes fill the air and burn the eyes of all spectators and inhabitants. The lava burns at 5000 degrees, but necessary. Some praise their safe distance, the weary ask what happened. It's always funny to hear the ungrateful wiping their eyes clear of ash. Complaining only after the smoke clears. The anger of the volcano the villagers all fear. They mourn those burned in treachery. An elder reminds them that the volcano's temper provides them with the very land in which they stand. Perception is king.

Loser's Limp

The harder I press the brakes, the faster I go. I glance in my rear view mirror. I see the car that I am driving chasing me. I swerve left to right. The man in the other car seems to be making gestures as if he is throwing things at me. "What's he throwing at me? I ask. An Old Man riding shotgun yells, "Chances, He's giving you chances." How stupid of him to think that I need anything he has! I curse at the old man. DISRESPECTFUL!

A car ahead of me cuts me off. I tighten my jaw, filled with rage. I give him the finger. OVERREACTION!

Aware of my high speed, I unfasten my seatbelt. RECKLESS! I'm eating pork, beef, grease, sugar and salt. GLUTTONY! Needles in my arms and legs, pills overflow from my pocket and fill my glove compartment. SELF-MEDICATION!

My Wife and Kids yell from the back seat. "SLOW DOWN!"

I tell everyone how tired I am. COP-OUT!

"You don't know how hard it is for me." SELF-PITY!

My last glance in the rear view shows no car chasing, no-one watching and no-one riding shotgun. I notice my Wife and Kids on the side of the road, watching me speed by. The road is coming to an end. I wipe my last tear, close my eyes and smile before I fall to my death.

The Old Man turns to my Wife and says, "That's all he wanted. My wife tells the children to leave as she asks the Old Man. "What did he want? The Old Man says, "PEACE". He just wanted to sleep.

Awakening

It was seen as a crime to deface a book.
I saw justice in tearing covers off books.
If not for covers, the words could be
free to roam our minds,
our hearts, our dreams.
My innocence led me to my bedside window.
The lure of wanting to see her.
Opportunities disguised as butterflies
dangle from the skies
and birds gather to see if anyone notices.

Her over We

She forgot the sun's favor. She forgot **her** aroma, **her** spectacle in the hearts of lovers near and far. How could she forget **her** position, **her** former length? She swayed enough to break **her** in half but never detached from the Earth.

Her petals spread out like wings announcing **her** arrival, if I should ever need **her**. She never asked for anything in return. And how did **we** repay **her**? Our driving force was lust and **we** used every inch of **her** for **her** beauty. **We** uprooted **her** from the ground with undeserving hands. **We** took from **her** and never gave back. She forgot how beautiful a flower should be. The mirror became a painful reminder of **her** past. She averted **her** eyes and lost herself in us. **We** are cursed by this selfishness and self-centeredness. **We** now must fill this endless hole in **her** center by reminding **her** every minute of **her** beauty. **We** must live our lives for **her**; our happiness is linked to **her**. **We** want the nice car for **her**, **we** want the nice house for **her**, **we** want the nice clothes for **her**, and **we** dress nicely for **her**. **We** must give back all that **we** took. **We** must now toss and turn on a bed of thorns, and pay our debt…to **her**.

Angels

So here I stand, looking up at you for
the first time. A slow soothing breeze
announces your arrival.
Feelings flow abundantly.
The sun shines on my heart, allowing
forward movement. There are no secrets
You will forever dwell in my memory.
On cloud nine with no fear of flying, or
should I say falling. I've heard your voice
I've heard your whispers I've heard your wings.

Treason

Once hungry but food is no longer an issue
His footsteps are heavy
Her breathing hurried
Blood stands still as a picture in its frame
His eyesight is a mirrored sunset
Movement paralyzed
Her stomach embodies a bottomless pit
His spit thickens
Her words hide
His palm sweats
The cut of her eyes
His contempt
Her regret
His scorn
Her disbelief
The sky whispers
The earth shakes
They realize that this isn't a dream
It's not a warning
It's not a punishment
It seems **betrayal** has kissed them

Observe

Are we all but shadows of flesh?
Are we the residue of former lives?
The blame of yesterday becoming
the fault of today,
Tomorrow yet unresolved in the
minds of the indigenous.
Time is forgotten in the eyes of the fool…
For time is a privilege in the eyes of the chosen.
When did word of mouth become life lessons?
The pen recites…the page remembers.
Nature keeps its promise of security.
The grass scans the ground.
The trees see all that is below.

Khem

The infinite, limitless darkness makes the distance from one's hand to one's face seem endless. There's magic in it, the unknown, the wonder. The beginning of things with no blemishes, scratches or scrapes. It's perfect. Each blink recharging darkness. Most people aren't afraid of the dark, but of themselves. A sleeping giant lies still in darkness. Alter egos hide in it. The light switch buys time. We buy time to run from ourselves, as if we can evade our shadows. As if opinions can't be judged. We look to the sky to blanket our questionable deeds and only look down when we fall.

Sounds of Deception

All hands on my chest, none at my back. That sounds like resistance to me. I should've known. It's really cold out here alone. I should've dressed warmer. Problems peek through gray clouds and pouring rain. I should've brought my umbrella. All windows and doors are locked when I need help. Looking forward to reaping what was sown. I should sit back and wait to be showered with payback. My heart initiating deeds without repayment in sight, it would be nice though. Maybe the game is war. I close my eyes and still hear the end. I close my ears and now I have become ignorant.

Overstood

I feel insulted when considered a writer.
If so, everyone who writes
should have consideration.
I write to hide my facial expressions.
I write when sound no longer matters.
Where only the eyes and the mind
of the reader can go.
I write to ignite your memory,
debate your inner voice.
My words become yours and burrow
into your memories.
I write to will a power that the sword never had.
My mind uses words as a vehicle,
Simply and oddly enough, driven by a thinker.

Destitute of Light

When discussing the unknown, or blindness. A bright light is the same as the dark if you cannot see. Too much light at one time forces you to close your eyes, making the darkness your refuge. We are all created in triple darkness in our mother's womb. Death brings us back to blackness as we lie silent in our "Mother Earth." On Earth the day is just as important as night. That is, if the self-righteous, arrogant, male chauvinist doesn't feel the need to manipulate time with this "daylight savings" trickery. Outside our planet there is blackness, seemingly infinite in our heavens. Why do we run from blackness? Does God need to see you lying within your mother to give you ten fingers and ten toes? Our brain sits in darkness and functions, our organs sit in darkness and function. Is physically seeing overrated? Do we believe only what we can see? If so, are the religious hypocrites? Or do we have so much faith in the unknown and so little faith in ourselves?

Win For Losing

It's like, the more I try, the more I cry. That house made of cards the way it crumbled. A hole in my pocket as freedom is some dollars and cents away. Almost as comfortable as thin soles on jagged rocks. I kneel to smell the roses after I've cut off my nose to spite my face.

It's like, the more I try, the more I cry. I watch humanity at the speed of light. All the babies that need to be held, yet I look around being the only person with arms. Stone shoes on glass floors, so useless, so loud, but every step confirms your existence. Necessary evils now appear. Your goals reach the sky, but you are afraid of heights. An elderly woman screams, "Hold your breath" as humanity watches the last tree fall.

It's like, the more I try, the more I cry. Animals watch humans and wonder who the animals really are. It's like, the longer you hold people up, the more they lose the use of their legs.

Becoming

The Heavens are clear; the rain has returned. The Sun shines for the first time, but still no forgiveness in sight. My yesterday shadows my now. Regrets tower over my intentions. I hold my tears behind my teeth. I am beneath the clouds in the sky, beneath the beginning of the ripple in a distant pond. Jousting with chances, becoming hopeful time after time, severed dreams between thoughts I have seen before. Words have no memory, no mercy, just energy. Surrounded by nothingness, I exist. Lessons that are learned through mistakes that seem to revisit unannounced pile sky high. Who becomes what they hope, what they dream, what they regret? Like a child, leaves that grow on a tree are innocent as long as its soil is sincere. The cold acts independently as a separate entity behind closed doors, but the absence of heat becomes its purpose. Positive or negative become the only two choices as light manifests itself. The storms that lie dormant inside some of us can push loved ones away. How can a storm protect itself from itself?

Daydreaming Pabulum

Pabulum 1

In those lights and cameras many resemble a deer stuck in headlights. It's not the fear that allows the deer to be struck and killed, it's curiosity.

Pabulum 2

To smile is to show my teeth
To smile is to stretch my lips
To smile is to loosen my jaws
To smile is to strengthen my gums
To smile is to hide
Why do we smile?

Pabulum 3

The cat that is stuck in the tree, although inconvenienced, escapes the flood. But a child freed from a forgotten womb is a walking corpse.

Pabulum 4

Do newborns bear new souls? Stars that have fallen and forgotten their place in the sky dream of home. They remember how they used to hide in blue skies. In jet black skies they flourished. That's the direct consequence of being given your identity on someone else's terms. Being told your existence but making you believe you're alone in galaxies. **To whose beat do we dance?**

Pabulum 5

Would one rather be kissed or hugged?
Would one rather be loved or respected?
Would one rather be missed or remembered?
The only catch is…you can't have both.

Pabulum 6

There are four people on earth responsible for populating the planet. There are two fertile women and two fertile men. They die and leave no children behind. Why?

Pabulum 7

So beautiful, so well built, great structure, fully furnished. The size of the backyard was breathtaking. I looked upstairs and to my dismay, no one was home.

Pabulum 8

Along with the light of truth, comes pain. What about those who say false lights are brighter, and combat pain with ecstasy? The witness is left blind.

Pabulum 9

The loser needs a little more help
The dying need a little more purpose
The devout need a little more fact
The martyr needs a little more time
The executive needs a little more humility
The beautiful need a little more reality

Pabulum 10

Trying to cheat time, I took the night away. But having no time to reflect at night put pressure on my day.

Pabulum 11

Convenience has found a way to complicate our lives. Airplanes, trains and automobiles are all convenient; however, people still walk.

Pabulum 12

Are raindrops content with their humble beginnings amongst the clouds, below the stars? Or are they disappointed to learn of their short and seemingly useless journey to the ground?

Pabulum 13

Are hours just seconds that have passed? Are years just a compilation of days? Are our lives just a series of events, fueled by a continuum of thoughts? Can we call these dreams? If the Earth is in constant rotation can there truly ever be forward movement? If our planet is suspended in mid-space, can we truly keep our heads out of the clouds?

Daydreaming's Why...

We daydream to laugh at the impossible. It's our "way out" of "Hell" and into the "Heaven" of our choice. It's our "out of body" experience, losing track of time and our surroundings. Lying dormant and underdeveloped as it tries every day to manifest itself into "God's suggestions." As we fancy places we've never gone to and remember all the things we've never done, we keep wondering. The Brain and the Mind are allies, not friends. The Heart and Feelings are roommates, not a couple. There isn't a beginning or an end. There is only time un-accounted for. There are only Daydreams. Just think…society views daydreaming as a waste of time.

Just as the camera records frames of your mind, long before your finger acts on impulse, I can see the state of things as they actually are. Acceptance of what is true and accurate, that which stays constant. I can now see what doesn't waiver. I can now come to terms with…

Reality

Realization

Has the day arrived where reality is negotiable? We sell the truth to the highest bidder and lose more. Perception argues his case that the sun rises and sets. Truth contests that the sun is stationary. Truth feels abandoned, taken for granted and unappreciated. I guess I can understand. The manipulation of perception sometimes goes unknown and therefore perception takes the form of truth. This misunderstanding brings war and hatred into the hearts of men and women, who in turn infect children with a bleached logic and we go like sand on a windy day. Who wins the game that no one plays? All who exist bear the burden of free will. What we feel is fragile and seals the door of life. Many find themselves bitter at those who have the keys.

Emotions

The light I now see is deeply woven in overstanding; I kneel in acceptance. The burden I bear is harsh. The things I know might make you not want to know me. I challenge you, testing everyone I come in contact with. Bats see in the dark, yet we see and still cannot. In the struggle of good, bad, right, and wrong, emotion is still the dilemma of the world. Two plus two equals four. Does your opinion or belief matter in this equation?

Apathy

We float higher and higher but no one notices. We shrug our shoulders looking into the eyes of inevitability. Two mirrors face one another. It's only inside out, not outside in. Does reality in this instance depend on your angle in the mirror? Is any angle real when eyeing only images? So if a tree falls and no one was there, did it fall? There are some who love to entertain double talk, while masking ignorance. Using complex jargon when they already have stated the obvious. The tree fell whether or not it was witnessed. Arrogance makes them question what takes place without their consent. The distance between the mountains and the stars is growing. The respect between man and his woman is shortening. We float higher and higher, away from that which does not change. **Reality.**

Enlightenment

I began my journey innocent and seduced by ignorance. I now open my eyes for the first time and see nothing. In fear for my existence I hide myself in the norm. The distraction of self draws me to others. The world owes me so much. The fight between good and evil resembles dependency. Depression is the reason I feed my hunger for entertainment. The strings of the puppet master are gone, but the hooks still remain. Habit is the driving force that breaks my will. My uncertainty breeds doubt and spawns fear. The unholy trinity of fear, uncertainty and doubt surrounds me at all times. My day depends on the weather and my looks drive me. I am so happy being unhappy and so comfortable being uncomfortable. I proudly and happily give the formula of my life to my children so they can prosper. The dead hate the living and the living seem to be already dead themselves.

Last Cry

This ink is cursed by a troubled messenger. Forced to drag my pen along this page and outline pain. I walk the path of the burdened. The impoverished must use caution when he asks; he may already have more than the giver. Fear is the bridge between here and there. We play in our pictures until they burn and curl in disbelief. No one is exempt from time. Rustling leaves to uncover the past, losing track of time spent, continuing where someone else left off. Pressure challenges my purpose. I answer the same question over and over again, yet they ask the same questions in their sleep. I was forced to forget my emotions so you can sell them back to me at a discount. Punishing and rewarding me with my own feelings. Whether I forget or remember, I somehow end up spending fool's gold. As long as my inner light shines, I am forced to deal, forced to make sense of non-sense.

The Unknower

One nation under God lies in a mint. So what lies beneath as hidden as snake's belly? Some appetites crave indifference. A whole nation absorbing garbage, whether you invite or invoke, the stench remains. The hand that once fed now bleeds nonstop. Houses fall like dominoes; the white jackets check the bricks not the foundation. You call that health care; I call that health careless. The disenfranchised are proud of what? The caterpillar that can't find its cocoon loses its destiny. Its beauty wasn't lost or gained, it lay dormant. A caterpillar with no purpose erases the butterfly. Its very existence would be questioned. A child with no memory has no future. His mother emptied and hollowed then filled with concrete. She takes a deep breath and they run for cover. Is that fear or respect? Five rings make you claim inconsistencies. The turkey that flew, the pig that kept a neat pen, the cow that ate meat. How absurd? But subconsciously wishing it were true to justify the lies we tell our children. Before one can **teach**, one must **learn**. Before one learns, one must **remember**. Before one can remember what was learned, so one can teach, he or she must first **care**.

Pressure

I've been forced unto the fire of accountability, forced to know it all. Trying your best is second fiddle and unacceptable. Beginning generations depend on your mistakes to stand, we hope, on solid ground in the future. No credit given. The arrogance of seeing yourself through others' eyes is overwhelming. There is nothing but sacrifice to be you. I wonder if they know the gamble of being loved in the beginning and judged in the end. How can you give love you never received? To teach things you were never taught. To one day see your transgressions in the deeds and actions of your offspring and know it may be too late to change it. How do you correct your flaws when you put your life on hold for 21 years? Passing on your fears and failures haunts every step you take. Meet the Parents.

The Chase

I was born with my purpose hidden
from me, harnessed by
those who hide bits and pieces of my lineage.
They then help me look, telling me
I'm warm but never hot.
In the house of 100 doors, they're all open.
The question isn't who opened them
It's which ones do we close.
Right needs wrong to live
Life needs death
Hate needs love Good needs evil.
Using space as my guide,
a beginning doesn't always need an end.
An empty cup is seemingly useless
but is such a great start.
Seeing colors and not actions has a
blinding effect.

Velvet

The umbilical cord was wrapped
around his neck; how did he live?
That bullet just missed his brain!
I opened my door and there was a baby at my
feet who grew up and saved me from poverty.
No money on my child's birthday…I asked "What do
you want today", he said
"I want you Daddy"!
These are the shoes he likes,
they said he would never walk.
They found their way through
a path covered with leaves
She found bloom beneath the
make-up covering her scars
She looked the rapist in the
eyes while on her back
She said in a soft voice "have fun"
A tear fell through his mask before
he got up and ran away.
No wrapping paper
No bows No special occasions
but
Gifts nonetheless.

Pang

Lying deep beneath the smiles
Deep beneath the beauty
Deep beneath the surface
Ageless, timeless it seems
Like a coward, pain hides and
resurfaces in our emotions
Memories act as carriers
They then change from a budding flower to
A book we close at our own discretion
A deck of cards we play with until
we're ready to deal.
Silent Pain, unknown to the victim until behavior
and body language shows me clues. The victim
blinks slowly, looking to me for advice and guidance.
All I can say is pain sometimes has no cure, no
season, no script, just tears… just tissue.

The Gimmies

It's so easy. No one will ever know
No one will miss it and if they know,
they won't care
It's the mystery in history
There is no second or runner up
I have enough time
I have enough resources
My army is strong enough
Clarity of stone over clarity of self
Quantity of life over quality of life
Brainwashed beyond all life and morality, that's
The motivation of a thief, the greed and
arrogance of a superpower…

The Twist

Clouds of fallen memories
Admire the sun's resolve
Children play in our mistakes
And we're too busy living
I ask the trees for forgiveness
As they stand by and say nothing
Birds fly so guilt-free, their wings extended
full capacity every flight
My reflection stares back at me,
two men talking – one man thinking
Limitless as a mother's love,
as a child's forgiveness
Trust and honesty never hold a
candle to dishonesty and distrust
The irony of the flesh

Asylum

Ignorance is so comforting. Seeming to disappear in it, sometimes I miss it and I wish I could go back. I would have so much popularity, so many friends. Normality maintains its edge over humanity. The ignorant sleep forever, the wise toss, turn, and pace. The rocks on their side of the street are jagged and dangerous. Ignorance faces opposition when those who were asleep are now awake. I haven't slept in about 17 years, probably never will. The fate I chose was my choice alone. I walk with my left foot forward on the same side as my heart. I bring my good intentions to the surface. I expel emotions of the worldly. I try hard unsettling. I feel alone most nights. I feel as endless as the sea looks, standing onshore. A journey I must take even if it kills me. With the ignorant sleep I travel safely, I travel swift, I'm focused. It's the weirdest thing the way they cry in their sleep, the ignorant, that is. My eyelids get heavy from time to time. I want to sleep sometimes but I remember my decision. I acknowledge the seduction of it all, the security of the ignorant. I refuse to ignore life's lessons. I refuse to step over my blessings and remain amongst the lost.

What a Web We Weave

Look at that smile. The children of children laugh endlessly. The innocence they display gives elders hope. What happens to God's children who become society's muses? They used never to leave your side, now they go missing. What have we done to our children? Those smiles become scarce. When did we trade toys for hugs? Our push for excellence must be stronger than the peer pressure that will soon push them. Save the babies. They walk with their hands out, willing to take our problems, our fears, our doubt, our outlook on life, our abuse, our shortcomings, our faults. Unable to see, they become us. Congratulations. They then have children. Congratulations. A teacher passes one question around a classroom. No one finds the answer, but they all graduate. Material things compensate for our shortcomings. We spread stories about a rabbit that lays eggs; a man who brings gifts all through the night, reaching every house in the world within hours and sliding down a chimney that most of us don't have; a little boy who shoots people in the backside to make them love; and a winged fairy that brings money when a tooth is lost. Then we dare them to lie to us. Children are our forgiveness, our second or third chance to ensure our life isn't theirs. Keep your money, the things in their life they hold on to are free. We shouldn't hate ourselves through our children. They need us. Maybe we'd rather they hate us. Like spoiled milk we shortly see the change. No smiles, no playing, no expressions on their faces. However, once they open their mouths we smell the stench of our neglect.

The Vanishing

The puppets suffer while the puppeteer prospers
Knowing that in their means to an end there lies a beginning He punished those who didn't flourish under his blue lights One must question all known, when it rolls down the hills of deception
The every-cloud-has-a-silver-lining person never looked up The grass-is-greener-on-the-other-side person stayed indoors The glass-half-full person wasn't thirsty
The love-everybody person hated himself
The pen sat in his highchair of conceit and pride over the sword...
Until he met the lens
The current in this society seems to be currency
What good is hearing without understanding?
What good is seeing without noticing?
The only thing worse is hearing, seeing, touching, tasting, but not believing.
This is the last true symptom of full-blown ignorance.

Callow

They say it's always darkest before the dawn,
Insanity differs in this reality,
Yet the truth is as evident as the air we breathe.
The apathy of the masses ensures that the truth escapes humanity
Just as water runs through an open palm.
The sun stands in the sky with no legs and reigns supreme in our skies.
The insane run from this and call their fear Global Warming. Then consume the teachings of the students of teachers.
What man has the power to erase memories and recreate yesterday?
Who made you respect the effect and not the cause? The blue people who thrive off moon energy
The insane don't know it.
Those who see their true colors are called insane.
Save yourself so you can save the children from having children.
Can you love everyone and hate yourself?
Restoration of balance, plus suppression of egos minus fantasy will bring peace.

Four Legs

To ask for the eggs, milk and flour back after the cake has risen may be too late but better late than never. Being caught, brought, bought and taught by those who caught, brought, bought and taught us invites déjà vu. Putting value on the valueless breaks the back of balance, paralyzing all fairness and equality. For he who made the law somehow flew above it, shattering the gavel. He tipped the scale that weighs hypocrisy full tilt. More price tags may lead to more toe tags. People look up to God, texting their prayers, as fingers now talk more than we do. Hugs will soon cause disease, as doctors inoculate the public against the public. If we're not careful, thinking will become extinct and this thoughtless age will consume the masses. This new age will take the life from the living and run us out of our right minds. "Only the strong survive" or "kill or be killed" is the savage logic by left mind thinkers. It is the nature of a man that distinguishes him. The nature of something can never be changed. What nature are you?

Fortune

Day after day, pain has become our God. Countless sessions of our unwilling worship become gospel. We sometimes find ourselves blindly reaching for happiness as if reaching for dust particles in the air as that one ray of sun goes astray. Many have been worshipping pain so long that happiness is distorted and becomes pleasure, overpowering their perception. Desperation of the soul fuels its restlessness, leaving impatience calling for a sedative. Pleasure in a happiness suit feels its acceptance justified regardless of morality. As sugar pours over our pain, true happiness drifts deeper into the unattainable, deeper into the distance, deeper into the shadows of bliss we fall.

Reality's Pabulum

Pabulum 14

We attempt to acquire unbelievable riches and have our picture over the mantelpiece. At our time of death, money and power are useless. I notice that most of the people who we remember and cherish took pride in having made us smile. Sometimes the rich die poor.

Pabulum 15

Fear is the deadliest animal known to man. If its bite isn't handled correctly, its poison can produce fear in an unborn child. Where did this animal come from? And how could it have bitten us all at one time or another?

Pabulum 16

A man asked a genie to make him a perfect partner. The man said she had to have: long hair, small feet, light skin, big butt, great breasts and a small waist. When he got home he saw a woman on his bed with all those physical characteristics. But when he touched her, she lay lifeless. He looked up and wept, "What is this?"

The genie asked, "Haven't I given you exactly what you asked for?"

Pabulum 17

How do you save those who willingly but unknowingly destroy themselves and their children?

Remove the smart phone.

Pabulum 18

When you don't respect yourself, you feel hopeless, empty, and purposeless. You want to die to escape hell. Suicide is too harsh, too sudden. You need something slower, so…

You **entertain** yourself.

Pabulum 19

The skies of denial are lit and we see, hear and speak no evil. The question isn't, What do you know?

The question is, Do you want to know?

Pabulum 20

Most people die within a ten-mile radius of where they were born and know at forty years old exactly what they knew at eighteen.

Has anyone ever been bitten by a book?

Pabulum 21

Throwing the core of an apple onto the ground is called littering and considered a crime. But the same people of authority decide to create a city dump and throw garbage on the ground. An apple core will go back into the Earth; however, concrete won't.

Which is littering?

Pabulum 22

Let's forgive our parents; they did the best they could. Let's forgive the sun for not shining every day. Let's forgive the rain for ruining our plans. Let's forgive our children for following our lead. Most importantly, let's forgive ourselves. Let's forgive our mistakes and bad decisions. Let's forgive our failed dreams or the loss of our will to chase them any longer.

Pabulum 23

Melt means: to pass or change or to fade gradually.

America's **melting pot** is an interesting concept, established in the 1780s to describe the assimilation of immigrants into America. It was supposedly meant to bring different elements together in a harmonious co-existence.

This concept requires much thought. One must ask why 198 different nationalities have to be changed, or must gradually fade away. Therefore, the **melting pot** concept should not take the focus away from the **Grand Chef** who is doing the cooking.

Reality's Why

One of the most manipulated forms of existence. The world we see in the back of our eyes that sees us all. "The right hand" of "Mother Nature" and the foundation of all decisions. Our purpose lives here, our beliefs live here, war with our common sense lives here, we take ownership of it and like clay we sometimes shape reality to fit our comfort levels. The reality of the atheist differs from the pastor. The reality of the historian may differ from the scientist. The heart of a person guides his/her intentions, which measures his/her spirituality, which reveals his/her reality. All that makes you insane can also free you. The rhetoric of straight lines never had a purpose in circles from which we are comprised. The blackness you hide from in turn hides you. And this reality may differ but I doubt it will ever change.

Of course you know, this means…

War

No Pardon

Sitting atop unsettled water, my contempt peaks. Three- fifths man surrounded by three-fourths water, home is as lost as I am right now. She bleeds and I watch her, I look the other way. My hatred consumes that coldness and keeps me human. Those roots burrow themselves in the sanctuary of our blessed soil and ask we pardon its wretched leaves. That pig, that whore of ideals, plagues our land and chases me to the sea. Guilt thickens your blood, yet your trickery secures your plate at my family's table. No horns, no hooves, you mask in desire. Pushing frantically through those doors when everything I want is behind me. Confusion, confusion, confusion is your weapon of choice. I anxiously wait atop these waters. I will drown the monster and disturb the sea bottom, where mercy had no home centuries ago.

Putrid

Blood and ash mix with dirt along our path. The stench of Cowards and their stripes are among us here. Those who are convinced that green-spun cotton ruled the minds and hearts of civility began their very own perversion. I can only cry and wait to be outnumbered by demons with heartbeats that share my womb. They ride atop machines and ambush women and children with confusion. To live in shame is as close to maggots that I pray to pull from the skulls of the putrid. Traitors hang high and bleed out. They die infinite deaths and are charged with infinite crimes in two different dimensions. For the vile of the Earth I shall beg the permission of the elders to swiftly cast judgment so I may present their innards before them. There isn't any refuge for the Putrid. The evil in you will be exposed once my blade cracks your filthy skin. When we arrive with our flag, we will feed your followers manure. Some say that the civilized must wait for soldiers that never come. Women too must wait for the husbands to stop courting whores so that they may hear their cries. For he's diluted, he's infected, he's addicted to subhuman doctrine from a cloudy, remote, cold, barren land. He's mislead, afraid and most of all wanted by me and my soldiers. God has no place for the putrid and there is no hole in this earth to rest in. His mother defiles her womb for laboring him.

For even rain can find its home once again at sea. God has heightened my sense of smell and has blessed my blade. I can track him from infinite distance and destroy him and anyone that sheds a tear for him.

War Posture

I see cowards everywhere, the real stand alone amongst mice. With my last breath, my last efforts against injustice I chase that rat, the yellow traitor. The worst crime is treason and I shall judge you. To slay your own brother amongst strangers, "no mercy" screams the village and examples must be made. In war there are no prisoners, no mercy. A last resort should be treated as such. I dare you to explain loving your enemy looking down a smoking barrel. Hang them high for 600 million, I share their blood. I share the same heart. One day I shall house us all. A family reunion, the sun massages my skin and recharges me. Sustains my mission to rid the coward of himself. Blood stains the ground of those who never ask to meet treachery. I bandage as many as I can, but I can't get the blood from under my nails. This must never happen again. It's not God's plan to kill the innocent. It's her plan to let soldiers like me see their death and vow to see no more.

Hero

The paths of men meet at warrior's road. The beginning is fragile but the end is righteous. The Gods give and take at will. Many spirits seem to be broken. The posture of a wall is needed but not given. They still seem unwilling to engage. All is lost as the knower suffers and becomes the forgotten. The hidden truth forces us to internally realign our destiny. War allows hate to roam freely amongst us. Past, present and future become our holy trinity. Inner battles must be conquered and challenge the passion of a warrior. When you allow the enemy to choose your battles you are not free, and you are NOT a MAN.

Five Stars

The sound of cannons deafens the closest ear. War bringing the stench of regret on every face I lead. I blink in slow motion. Were there choices for these young men? How do you tell beaten men to give more of their life to death? I tell a tale of triumph to sway the wandering eye. My scope is in death's focus. I'm interrupted by a pipe bomb a hundred feet from me ripping into two 18-year-old kids. I take cover. Can I lead and cry? Wanting to run I dump every iron round my clip carries. I raise my right hand to pause our righteous onslaught, mustn't give away our position. You can't fight for life if you haven't embraced death. I have delusions of tucking my daughters into bed. The black water reminds me of my wife's hair. Soldiers cry out "Sir!, sir!…We must move, Sir, our position may be compromised!" I awaken from my dreams. "Right Here!" I yell. "Right here!" "Sir, I don't understand" yells a draftee fresh out of high school, ears still ringing from all the noise of death. "This is our position," I yell, knowing there is no way out. I walk in righteous steps cursed with knowledge, burdened with truth. "Who stands with me?" I yell. "Who stands with me?" I pump rounds into the forest, moving leaves aside so our bullets have no resistance en route to our enemies. I give up our position, bullets whiz through their helmets resembling a woodpecker in a tree. I aim at everything moving. The vibration of the trigger jolts my spine. We're surrounded. As my men fall to the ground I thank them for their sacrifice. I thank their families for raising men who were willing to lay their lives on the line. I notice a buzzing noise that can only be heard when my gun is empty. I awaken from my rage; all my men are gone. I'm the last man standing. But men we were, and as men we will be remembered.

Exceed

I go blank as I momentarily feed my desires, the worst of all emotion when under developed. After having my fill of the poison of my choice, I hang my head in shame. Addiction fills the air, one drag at a time, one drink at a time, one bite at a time. It's never enough pleasure, but always enough pain to sustain that refuge. Covering the problem and exposing my weakness at the same time. No matter who can or can't see my pain, I can't see the end. Anger turned inward fuels my dysfunctional behavior and raises the barrier between me and enlightenment. Escaping pain is the battle, but finding the source of the pain is the war.

Charge

Before there was darkness there was a purpose. That purpose swam to its egg and fought with every inch of its body for a chance to exist. Millions more with that same purpose soon followed. This fight for position lasted for days until the "Great Elders" whispered his name and gave him perfection in darkness, no sin. His "Mother God" gave him life. His first breath ensured him humility and freedom living by nature's standards. Family and community governed his world. He soon had a family of his own. With his child's first breath humility and freedom was promised as well. As a father and husband he promised his life and loyalty to his God, Elders, family, land and community. If his humility was taken, freedom taken, children killed or hurt, wife raped, God demonized, Elders disgraced, family separated, land stolen and his community burned to the ground, should he not be angry? The ingredients for war have been compiled. He gathered everyone he could. He sharpened every axe, knife and sword he could find. They ran as fast as they could to the battlegrounds. They faced death easily because in their hearts they will not be killed. Real men and women with the right to defend everything they loved. No savages among them, no slaves, only free men and women. If they fought for life in the beginning, then they must fight for life until the end.

The Switch

A smoking shoe lies miles from the owner. Innocent or guilty eyes remain open. Hot smoke rises from hatred faster than any conscience can feel. Casualty meets culture on this day. The ground felt everything, the sky witnessed everything, the trees stood by and said nothing. Fire burned the carnage, water split into droplets to wash away every square inch of death, then the wind blew it all away as if it never happened. The land can now be renamed, reassigned and re-cultured by offenders whose children can claim innocence of their bloodline's sins and enjoy ripe fruit from stolen seeds. Books will make heroes from hatred; they will make victims into rebels and savages. The slaughter will soon be taught to few survivors who will soon be honored to be slaves. Can a war be won? When defeated in war, the opposing side can retreat. Hopefully they gain strength and numbers to push forward once again. But when centuries pass of murdered grandfathers of murdered fathers of murdered sons who are all from murdered mothers, never think of revenge or justice in any way. That was a slaughter not a war.

War's Pabulum

Pabulum 24

I know I have semi-automatic weapons and grenades on my beltline. I've also brought planes with me that are dropping bombs on your land periodically killing innocent men, women and children. But I promise you that I come in peace.

Pabulum 25

Does turning the other cheek always show righteous restraint or am I sometimes submitting to invaders?

Pabulum 26

Anger + Ignorance + Greed = War
Reason + Intelligence + Diplomacy = A solution

Pabulum 27

Empty shells, smoking guns, and shiny
medals only a shoulder can see.
No soldiers, just minions
No purpose, just orders.

Pabulum 28

Fumes and spirits rise higher than any bird can soar. Hands bring about lifelessness in the fields. The ears never stop ringing and bullets cannot compare when entering the brain as an unwanted memory. Hopefully, one day the birds will forgive us all and fly again.

Pabulum 29

The only way to hide a square behind a circle is by having a very big circle. The only way to hide greed behind a war is to cover it with the hopes of peace.

Pabulum 30

The story after the war is the prize. Each side loses lives. Each side believes its cause is righteous.

Pabulum 31

I wonder which is worse, a warrior dressed in honor and war paint with no battle to attend or a battle rich in reason and right with no warriors standing at all.

War's Why...

Absolutely no other options are present. It is the most extreme resolution and strategy. Having tons of hidden agendas, it hides behind haste and rushed judgment. In war your mother is to be executed if she betrays the agenda. War should be waged on all intruders. Never negotiate with a thief over how much of your possessions he or she can keep. War's existence is questionable in societies with hearts and minds that are human. Millions of mirrors that show millions of reflections with millions of savages that stare into them and unfortunately repeating millions of years of savagery. At its foundation lies the concrete of conquest: ego, greed, envy, hatred and dissatisfaction. Peace talk and higher means of resolution must never be discussed with warmongers. Your optimism will be met with lead!

Listening to a wave crash silently on a secluded beach, basic relaxation can be none without her. Happiness that's forever, her sickness isn't acceptable. I'll run the farthest length and distance to find a cure. It's the least I can do for a soul and smile so pure. Although it's fun, two beings become one. No sorrow. Without her there's no tomorrow. A wilted dying flower in the garden, love that hardens is incurable, however, one true love is essential. Watched from the light above, we shine clean like doves. Many sleepless nights, loss of appetite. Some would say that this is…

Love

SG3

At times this God-forsaken place called Earth is dangerous, nothing like where you are now. Everyone was once where you are now. Unfortunately, it's been so long I've forgotten the smell, the feeling of triple darkness. Your time will soon be up there, I will have to keep you just as safe as you were. I will shape your reality. I'll take chunks of this world and blend them for your consumption of understanding. I must build your past, teaching you what you have forgotten. I will teach you to act on impulses unseen and unknown. I began your creation, yet my contact is delayed for nine months. Unfair? No. I need time to prepare for a lifetime of teaching. Patience will be my pillar. It's funny that no matter how tired, how sleepy, weary or heading for the grave, one still blinks effortlessly without thought. This lets me know there's always room, always a chance to gain your trust and your love. I anxiously await your arrival. **A letter to my unborn son**

Fool's Gold

The candle embodies love. The flame is the key because at this beginning point, love begins. The flame is lit. The longer the flame lasts the more it melts the relationship. New moments and challenges are beautiful but take time. Remember, time melts all candles. The life of the candle or relationship moves on and the candle takes on a new shape much different from its beginning. That flame of love is the catalyst initiating change and putting wear and tear on the wax or the relationship. Each time trying to co-exist, longing to find the flame that never extinguishes. Unfortunately, all candles burn out. Fortunately, there are a lot of candles in the world to choose. Unbeknownst to the couple, the candle burns never to be extinguished, it just needs something to devour, so it chooses wax. It's ironic that we seem to offer our bodies for love to devour.

Tickled

She became a rainbow that suddenly appears and lasts forever. The sound of violins playing softly carries along calm waters. She is a rose that buds and never wilts. A bird that takes flight and never lands; a sun that never sets, only rising to the singing of nature, as innocent as the smile of a child; food in the hands of the hungry; rest in the hearts and minds of the restless; the joy of a child's first steps or words brought to new parents, as the first kiss from your first love. This is how she makes me feel.

Inspiration

The promise that I vow never to break. The fragrance of bliss by which I'll forever inhale, the wink of the sun for half a split second making me eternally grateful. My reason, a calm breeze, the leaves on the tree that play all day, my clarity, my triumph, my treasure hidden from all thieves. My desire, my previous life, my feet touching the limits of heaven, my focus through the woods at night on foreign soil, my watchtower, my first breath outside my mother's womb, my last breath before my journey through eternity, my refuge from pain, my miss you, my need you, my want you.

Daze

Two people love each other but never met each other. Each knows the other in their dreams. They think from time to time about one another. As their thoughts travel they smile and look to the sky. For even though they sit on opposite sides of the Earth they see the same moon. It takes them back to their childhood. She remembers thinking that rainbows were candy, justifying her desperate attempt to touch one standing on the roof of her aunt's house.

If only she were taller she could reach that rainbow. She imagines tearing a piece from it and watching the colors drip down her wrist and onto her Sunday dress. He remembers the roar of the skies before a storm. Of course he thought he had done something wrong when the storm came. He would grab his puppy Oliver, a flashlight and his lucky quarter, and hide. In the shed he would reveal to Oliver that the rain was really falling stars and whatever he had done he would never do again. Two people who love each other but had never met each other. Just might if they keep their heads in the clouds.

Frenzy

I know it's getting late but don't leave before you get lost in us. Let me indulge you, nurture us for a while. Our surroundings seem to fade. Let's leave time behind us. Lock the door and throw away the key holding discretion prisoner. Let trust be my foreplay as I lay you down in comfortability. To need you now isn't soon enough. Forever isn't long enough. I would give anything to sit under your brown skies, become bliss, become selfless, and become addicted. When you arrive at the highpoint, that hidden ecstasy that you've found, that forbidden fruit that you've consumed and scream out, I hope pain isn't the villain.

Impulse

One man, one woman meet at a random time in an unfamiliar location. They know nothing about each other: their names a mystery; their lifestyle, background and favorite foods unknown and unimportant. They meet at different locations every day. They speak on a range of different topics. When seated in one of many different restaurants, they frequently change seating arrangements. They order different food every visit, regardless of taste. They can't judge one another. They remain spontaneous, guilt-free and live constantly in the moment. They walk away from the world with the wind at their backs. They are free, they are selfless, they're beyond love, and they are INFINITE.

Resistance

What will it take to love you? What about a smile? The scene of love, my wallet is out ready to pay the price, my napkin in hand ready to wipe the tears. Your eyes show me my imperfections and line them up for correction. What will it take to co-exist with you? Knowing I will never keep you. To keep is so possessive, so selfish, almost clipping the wings of a butterfly. That spirit is so perfect and free. For it belongs to humanity. For it belongs in my memory forever. I extend my arms to you to breathe. I lie with you until every inch of my skin is satisfied. You are perfection intensified. If only I could tell you with words. If only I could show you with action. The entrance of elation awaits, Chest to chest too far away. I will absorb every second of you, even if it's my last.

Untouchable

I too have exchanged a need for a want, the worst of all love crimes that bears the worst of all outcomes. I thought I could drink water from a different glass and get a different taste. I often found myself torn between trying to be happy or maintaining normality. Beauty became my burden. Those that said we couldn't put me in a cage. I forgot to live, I forgot my purpose. I got lost in us. When will we step back and realize that many of us do not love, we are living our entire lives looking for it. Love is an expansion. It's all around us and as invisible as the air we breathe. What is there to look for? It's not that we can't find love; we turn our back on it. Like I said, we exchange needs for wants, which happens to be the worst of all love crimes.

Sunset

I had a dream that was you, a happy ending before the beginning. I prematurely gave you my breath and my heart, knowing that you already had your own. You became my personal project. I took my hands and sculpted my concept of love. I nurtured you, gave you just the right amount of sunlight that would ensure your emotional growth. I put you in the clouds knowing that I couldn't fly. I put you so far ahead of me that you soon faded from my sight. They saw a fool but…I saw a chance.

Southeast

I now break my silence. I'm lost in the woods of betrayal, searching for a face to trust. I walk naked and barefoot along a trail of jagged sharp rocks. Confused by a pain other than bloody feet. A pain caused by a traitor I once loved. In agony I hold my breath and hear only my heartbeat. The only smile I have left appears to show me that my heart still beats unharmed. I am unable to reach the blade, so I leave it in hoping for the pain to stop. Emotions run wild; memories and revenge sway me from my path. Trees hear me yell in solitude. For the first time in a decade I'm alone. Each step making the blade heavier, each step counting down time. Those waters ahead remind me of my love. Once soothing in nature, now a forbidden drink I dare not taste. I look down only to notice that I've strayed off my path. How do I get back? Do I want to come back? Drowning in emotions, I find peace in noticing that through all the pain and suffering, I never took one step back.

Loathe

There's nothing more alarming than the taste of your own blood. I unknowingly bit into my lip but felt no pain.
I hate you, too!
You actor…as if those tears move me…as if you loved me more than you loved you. As if you have the right to hate anyone other than yourself and your actions. You relinquished your right to hate! You can't hate that which you need!!!!
A rose can't hate the stem on which it stands!
A blade of grass can't hate the soil from which it grows! You hate the fact that you can never hate me as much as I hate you.
I won't come down to your level…I cannot, it's impossible. If I were to do that I would have to crawl, slither on my belly, for that is your nature.
Huh…you hate me?
What nerve to say it with conviction as you narrow the slit in your face?
As if I'm the villain in your treacherous tale.
Your tongue should be cut out with the speed of the first glance in which I initially noticed those lying eyes of yours. May it fall at your feet and echo my hate for you through eternity, through all walls that stand. I curse the womb that carried you. I hate the penis that initiated conception. and if you cut your eyes at me again I'm going to…you…you know what? Goodbye!

The Veil

I was told to never talk to strangers. If I had followed those instructions, I would have no friends and no companion. We are all strangers until we see an opportunity to make the stranger a friend, wife or husband. That warm feeling that slowly moves up your spine quickly moves him or her out of stranger territory. You wonder how they could have ever been strangers now that they have become a part of you. You wonder what you would have been missing had you listened. However, time has a funny way of exposing trickery if you are fortunate enough to notice the change. It's very important not to misunderstand the message; it's not the person as much as their intentions you need to avoid. You must check your intentions as well, because you are a stranger to them. Always remember that the skill of choosing one's company is a blessing from God and time. The most difficult obstacle is that evil intentions never hide behind frowns, but smiles.

Fancy

They say it's better to have loved and lost than never to have loved at all.
What if it was never love? Then what did you lose?
Love's infinite energy Only a few ever drink these waters
Breathe that air Eyes wide open to see love's shadow for their own personal
extension Loving your neighbor must first begin with your reflection Like a star she brightens my skies and awakens love's purpose To be seen in action, words provide the smoke screen for deceit Beauty sets the stage
Optimism and insecurity, the deadliest love potion, close
the show. The love you boast of is based on your hopes and dreams The picture you paint that you hope becomes prophecy
Your love is primarily your ego The battle to love others is your futile attempt to love yourself
As a result, love remains, **unattained**

The Battery, the Rose and the Rain

Trying so hard to live I almost died. I jumped into blindness by having only a happy ending in sight. Wanting so badly to be more than what others saw of me. Wanting that security of nothingness, vanity engulfed me. Insecurity somehow played another role in the destruction of the chemistry between my eyes and my heart. I sacrificed everything for a little bit of nothing. When you enter into a union between yourself and the superficial, you will always pay a heavy ransom. When we step back from the ocean we only see blue, but in the eye of the storm I saw only survival. I tried with all my time. I tried with all my experience. Youth made every attempt toward sanity seem unreachable. My love seemed to bounce off every mirror I glanced into. Walking through that dark alley, I found the strength to push through tissue paper disguised as a brick wall. A dead- end flooded with my tears. Experience is now my lifeline. Trying so hard to live, I almost died and by trying so hard to stay, I simply moved on.

Love's Pabulum

Pabulum 32

Lust fills these four walls, now that our eyes have met Nothing matters at desperation's core
Breathing intensifies, hearts race, sweat beads and our legs tangle.
Children will forever cover their eyes and ears after this. What happens after we start? What happens if we cannot stop?

Pabulum 33

Life is living in courage when the world lives in fear. Life is having someone to die for, something to hope for and enough time and wisdom to know the difference. Life is changing someone's diaper and hoping one day they'll return the favor.

Pabulum 34

He didn't cheat on his wife for the hell of it. He didn't cheat on his wife for sport. Lust wasn't his driving force. He cheated on his wife because he couldn't understand what his wife could see in him to love.

Pabulum 35

The only goal in your relationship shouldn't be to stay in one.

Pabulum 36

A woman wants to love; a man loves what he wants.

Pabulum 37

Can two people who are emotionally and spiritually weak separately become emotionally and spiritually strong together?

Pabulum 38

"Why do you love me"? She asked,
"because I love me," He replied.

Meet the trophy. A woman rooted only in vanity allows a man to masturbate. He consciously has sex with her, but subconsciously has sex with himself by way of his ego.

Pabulum 39

Love must be very small because people always seem to lose it or they're always trying to find it. Maybe it's a ditch, seeming as people fall in and out of it. Well good luck hoping that love will find you, they say it's blind. The problem is its twin brother, lust.
People always mix them up.

Pabulum 40

I once knew a girl who was desperately looking for something. No one ever told her what to look for or why she needed it. To this day I don't know if she ever **found** what she was looking for.

But I do know she **los**t what she had.

Pabulum 41

Looking for someone to love you?
Looking for someone to love?
Go in the bathroom
Stand in front of the sink
Turn on the light
Yes, the ultimate love.

Pabulum 42

He felt compelled to tell her that she had the most beautiful eyes he had **ever** seen. She felt compelled to tell him that he had the most beautiful eyes she had **never** seen…

because she was blind.

Pabulum 43

The opposite of love isn't hate. The opposite of love is apathy, not caring either way.

Pabulum 44

Fire kills and destroys people and property every day. However, fire cooks our meals and heats our homes in the winter. Hate is one of the most powerful and misunderstood emotions. Hate and ignorance can destroy the World, but hate and righteousness can help us preserve the World we love.

Pabulum 45

She said she was hungry, so I offered her food.
She didn't want food.
She said she was building, so I offered her tools.
She didn't want tools.
In desperation, I called her mother and asked her,
What should I do?
Her mother answered, She does want those things
She just doesn't want **you**.

Love's Why

We spend our entire lives trying to be on love's VIP list, a trip worth hiking, climbing, swimming, and flying to get to. Either we are looking in the wrong places or we don't have a clue what to look for. It hides from the desperate and runs from the arrogant. Those who find it can't seem to hold onto it. Some get frustrated and lose hope. It's hard to expect answers from those who are lost in the same forest. The beloved know that respect is the house that keeps love safe and in arm's reach. I wonder if companionship is the destination and love is the engine that will carry us. Our inability to properly receive or reciprocate love is our disconnection to nature. Humanity's relationship with nature is our relationship to the planet Earth. As long as we overlook this major detail, love of any kind will remain out of view. Insecurities and synthetic ideals can work love at such a speed only light can imagine. The very thing that puts love in such high demand is to blame for its inevitable extinction. It makes hugs lie. It gives free spirits alien purposes. It should be an unspoken word, so that it may stay a while.

Now let us…

Pray

Petition

(To the universal God I pray)

I pray… for pure energy that is the source of the "ALL". The founding energy that has no name, the energy that creates and destroys without bias, the energy that isn't jealous or vindictive, the energy that doesn't curse or judge, the energy that originated in simplicity, that time before history began, the energy that used all religions as an extension of itself for the common good of humanity. This founding benevolent energy that watched close by as each finger broke away from its righteous hand and began judging each other. Corruption of sincerity and truth soon created an alien dynamic called "fear".

I pray for children born of parents that were never found.

I pray for the smallest part in all of us that is whole.

I pray for food in the stomachs of the hungry.

I pray for forgiveness in the heart of the victim.

I pray that I am ready for the answers to my questions.

I pray for civility and diplomacy before war.

I pray for you **I pray** for them **I pray** for me.

Prayer 1

Most High, please bless the one with nowhere to call home. No food to fill, water to spill, and all alone. No clothes to wear, love to spare, what a way to live. Roaming without any destination, no friends, no family, what a way to live, what a fate to bear.

Most High, please bless the one with no one for whom to care. Most High, please bless the one whose blessings aren't there.

Prayer 2

Even though I walk in the company of the humanoid invaders, I fear not their evil. My ancestors walk with me. My knowledge and my sword they comfort me. My blessings overflow, surely goodness and mercy shall follow me for eternity and I will dwell amongst those who came before me within sight of the ALL.

Prayer 3

Now I lay me down to sleep. I command safe spirits amongst my family. If I should travel and never wake, don't cry, there's no such thing as "die." I will live in righteousness and die for freedom and justice. Goodnight, my son.

Prayer's Pabulum

Pabulum 46

I am ready and willing and hopefully not forsaken.

If the lord is ready to giveth, I am surely ready to taketh.

Pabulum 47

"So because you are lukewarm – neither hot or cold, I will spit you out."

Revelation 3:16

Good luck sitting on that fence.

Pabulum 48

"Thy Kingdom come, Thy will be done,
on Earth as it is in Heaven"

Who told us **we must die** to get to Heaven?

Pabulum 49

It is said that no matter what you do, if you are truly sorry forgiveness will be granted. I know from personal experience that all who want forgiveness are always truly sorry until their next transgression. However, Adam and Eve made **one mistake** and were banished from God's favor **forever.** I'm sure they were very sorry. They received **no second chance.** Lot's wife, in The Book of Genesis, was told not to look back at the destruction of Sodom and Gomorra. She also made **one mistake** by looking back and became a pillar of salt **forever.** Lot's wife was given **no second chance.**

Where do we receive these infinite chances of forgiveness?

Pabulum 50

God gave man a brain and with that great gift, a chance to become a God himself. Unfortunately, when God gave man a penis he became a fool.

Pabulum 51

It is said that God created a woman from a man. However, every man on the planet has a navel. Which would probably mean that an umbilical cord had been attached there, which would probably mean that all men come from women.

I wonder when the creation story changed.

Pabulum 52

The weak and dependent nations pray for their enemy. The informed, prosperous and leading nations pray for the strength to destroy their enemy.

Pabulum 53

A **version** is an interpretation of a matter from a particular viewpoint.
A **viewpoint** is a mental position or point of view.

There are at least 15 different versions of the Bible which were sanctioned by several different people. The King James Version is one of the most popular versions.

Are we following God's words or the opinions, viewpoints and interpretations of men? One must ask.

Pabulum 54

Would you like to have a book that had pages missing from it? Would you like to have a book with chapters missing?

If you purchased such a book, how would you realize the author's vision?

My guess is that the reader would want full access to the complete story of the book. If one paragraph is missing it could compromise the validity of book and the story as a whole.

155,683 words, 5,700 verses, and 168 chapters are missing from the Bible.
The authenticity of these writings was deemed questionable and hence removed.

Who has the right to change or remove "God's" words?
What was left for faithful followers to read?

Pabulum 55

There are over 2.2 billion Christians or people accepting Jesus Christ as their Lord and savior. It's unfair that a group of men control and manipulate the words that so many people believe are the words of God. How long have they been changing concepts? How long have they been "playing God"?

Pabulum 56

"Seek and you shall find"
Mathew7:7

There are too many sources of information for us to wander in the dark. We must find righteous truth by unmasking lies. God knows that if the truth was in front of us we wouldn't need to look, the truth must be hidden somewhere. Therefore, analyzing and asking questions for better clarity should never be called sacrilegious.

Pabulum 57

Prove all things; hold fast that which is good.
KJV 1Thessalonians 5:21

To prove: To establish the truth or, to establish authenticity or validity, subject to a test, comparison or analysis, to determine quality or acceptability or to verify correctness.

Pabulum 58

"The prudent man looks well, **but the fool believeth every word.**"

Proverbs 14:15

To be prudent: to be sensible, to be wise or careful, exercising good judgment or common sense.

Pabulum 59

Heaven is the recognition and acceptance of beauty all around us, even though it may seem that we are in Hell.

"I can't make it rain or snow or create the petal of a rose. I know there is some force out there responsible. If you choose to call that power Jesus Christ or ALLAH, that's up to you. I choose to respect it, without necessarily calling it anything."

Dr. John Henrik Clarke

Prayers Why

I do believe that at the root of all organized religions there lies the hope of enlightenment and self-mastery. We have a chance to understand a greater power and live in harmony with nature. I'm often troubled when sacred teachings are used to support the agendas of men and not reciprocity. Some kneel or bend down while others may stand. Regardless of the ritual, all prayers are sent up to the heavens. Should we pray for riches? Or pray for others' prosperity? Should we pray for forgiveness? Should we pray for the patience to forgive others? Faith is having sight without seeing and knowledge without knowing. I wonder how any faith can judge another when we all seem to not see or know anything for certain. Once we develop the ability to love selflessly, respect our mind, body, nature, family and neighbor, our prayers have already been answered. Fear of damnation that leads to good deeds is faithless.

Have some more…

The Binge

Keepsake

Women wept in the presence of Marcus the Conqueror. He loved to hear them cry out in passion. It filled him with air, it fed his thirst for more, and it fueled his deep desire to drive a flag into their center claiming his omnipotence. It secured his dominance. At that moment, when the women were at their most vulnerable point, they would reveal their innermost agony. The fear of living without love seemed to haunt them. He soon would learn the difference between pain and pleasure.

The next woman he claimed wept; however, this time it disturbed him. It was so loud it gave him a headache. He jumped and asked, "Why so loud?" But the woman looked puzzled. She gave no answer so he tried to continue. The next time she wept but this time it seemed louder than ever. It took all the pleasure out of their love-making. He jumped up and got dressed. To her dismay. She asked "What's wrong?" He looked at her with contempt then said, "You, psycho!" As he dressed the woman had that same puzzled look on her face, trying to figure out why he was so upset. He couldn't help feeling unfulfilled. He needed to indulge again.

He called another woman and another. One after the other he heard nothing but crying and yelling. The last woman felt the sharp blade of his frustration. "GET OUT!" Again that puzzled look, wondering why he was having an outburst. As the door closed behind her, he fell to his bed in exhaustion. He lay looking at the ceiling.

Sweat pouredfrom his body as he wondered what has happened and why were these women so miserable?

KNOCK, KNOCK at the door.

"Who is it?"

"It's me man, Mike!" His childhood friend.

"Come in, it's open!"

"Hey man, put some clothes on!"

He had forgotten he was naked.

"Are you alright?" Mike asks.

"I'm OK man, what's up with this pop-up visit?"

"I have this porno movie I wanted you to see, man!"

"You came all this way to show me a porn, Mike?" Disbelief.

"You make it sound so dirty."

Five minutes into the movie Marcus shouts, "Turn this shit off, Mike!"

"What's wrong man? Calm down, you don't like women no more?"

"How can you watch this with all those women yelling and screaming?" Marcus asks.

"What are you talking about?"

"They're not enjoying one bit of that!"

"Are you serious?" Mike asks.

In disbelief, Marcus asks, "You don't see or hear that?

"Hell no!" says Mike.

Marcus stares at floor. "What's going on with me?" he asks himself, then, remembering Mike, says, "Come by a little later man, I have to figure some things out."

"You're kicking me out?" asks Mike. "Give me my movie! I'm going where me and my movie are appreciated!" After Mike leaves, Marcus goes to put some water on his face. As the water runs through his fingers, he starts to cry. He splashes the water on his face. Reaching for a towel it is handed to him. He screams, wipes his face, jumps back and throws punches in every direction before hitting the ground. As his eyes focus he sees a woman dressed in white, who stands about 5' 8". She has beautiful brown skin. He can't help himself, he has to tell her something. "You are beautiful!" Snapping out of his attraction, he asks "how did you get in here?" as he looks around and sees no forced entry. "You are asking all of the wrong questions," she replies.

"The right question would be, why am I here?

"Why do you make claims of my beauty? Is that all you see?" she asks.

"Listen, you're in my house and I didn't invite you, please answer my questions before I call the police!"

"What is your name?"

"If you must know, my name is Matira, Maat Hi Priestess and general of the East Armies."

"Does this have anything to do with these screaming women?" Marcus asks desperately.

"Your concept of beauty has one side. It's confined to the physical, not knowing of the mental, spiritual, metaphysical and multidimensional."

"What the hell are you talking about?" he asks.

"You are a "Barek warrior", Marcus, both man and God," says Matira.

"If I had known you were coming I would have popped some popcorn, this stuff is rich!" he replies laughing.

Matira is expressionless. "Look in the mirror," she says. "You're very handsome, women can't resist you. Has any woman in your whole life ever turned you down?"

"No, never," he replies.

"You thought that the women were crying because you were "good" huh?" she asks.

"But, of course." Arrogantly.

"How many times have woman cried during sex?"

"All my life." He looks as though things are starting to make sense.

"But you have noticed that the screams have gotten louder and unbearable?" she asks.

"Yeah, what's going on?"

"The great war has come full circle. Marcus, you must claim your true identity as the 'safe keeper of women's souls'. The Earth is in danger."

"Danger?" he asks.

"The woman is the life giver and she is now buried in the role of sex servitude and male chauvinism. Her womb doesn't only incubate life, there was a self-destruct mechanism placed there by the Elders. If their hurt souls aren't aided and revitalized, their wombs will sync and detonate the planet. This was the sacred pact of the Elders, to ensure that the creators of life will always be respected."

"What can I do?" Marcus asks.

The Priestess Matira puts out her hand, "Come with me." Looking intensely into his eyes she says, "I must warn you that as we jump dimensions and worlds, your concept of beauty and sexual power will change dramatically."

Then an explosion to the left of Marcus blows him back. Matira looks to the source of the explosion, "Goat head Vikings, they must have followed me through the portal."

One of the creatures tries to attack her. She steps back, draws her sword and beheads it!

"We must go now! Take my hand!" she yells. "OK" he says.

To be continued…

What it seems

A man stood up in class and asked his college professor if there was a hell. "I've seen hell, I see it every day," the professor replied. "I have seen its inhabitants. I was given a tour. Hell has been transformed beyond death to the living.'" "I've seen the eavesdropper and the gossips made blind, with ears made so sensitive that the blink of one's eye sounded like an explosion. The greedy given bottomless stomachs, tormented by having hunger unfulfilled. The supermodel tormented with clothes that never fitted; every piece four sizes too small. Those who have lived a life based on vanity given mirrors that only amplified their imperfections.

"I've seen the oil and the diamond tycoon fed that which brought them riches. Oil was pumped into him until it poured from his eyes, diamonds were forced down his throat, cutting every organ. The cigarette billionaire inhaling nails for eternity.

"The cowards who lived their whole life in the presence of injustice, lined up in two rows and blindfolded, fire placed at their feet. Every time they tried to run, the Demon lords would stab them. Now they were forced to stand their ground.

"It seems that the way we live chooses our eternity. It makes 'what comes around goes around' truly, a golden rule."

The student asked sarcastically, "Why do you know so much about hell and how do you come and go as you please?"

The professor replied, "Well, I was so fascinated with the walls of hell he made me its eternal tour guide. But I never leave."

"What do you mean, you never leave? If you never leave, how are you here right now?"

The student then gasped, "What are you trying to say? That we are Hell's next batch of sinners?"

The class let out a roar of laughter, but the professor said nothing. He got up from his seat, locked the windows and the doors. "Who is this man that you are referring to?" the student asked with a blank look on his face. The lights then extinguished and only the so-called professor's voice could be heard:

"He has many names."

The Loudest Whisper

I used to rule my world, only a ladder could reach my throne. I led those who followed. Drums and trumpets echoed throughout my holy of holies. Laughter of adults and children were the same. Honesty above my brow, respect at my feet when I ruled my world. The whispering stranger changed everything.

A hooded stranger invisible to the sun, his eyes resembled the ocean. Deception his armor, secrecy his shield and envy his sword. One by one he whispered to the children. Using unseen communication as subliminal suggestion, he never said a word. Laughter soon became a memory. The skin of drums became dry and brittle. Horns soon faded as my throne descended closer to the ground.

One night the stranger visited my bedside. "I am the new King," he whispered.

"They will never follow you," I yelled.

"They already do," he claimed. He continued, "You give them reality and freedom, I give them vanity and fantasy." The stranger said nothing more. I heard only deep breathing and could see his breath leave his hood. I slept, hoping that this stranger would just go away.

When I awoke the next morning, I walked to my balcony and no longer felt his presence in my nation's lands. I looked to my left, where I place my crown, and it was gone. I frantically got dressed, left my home and walked amongst my people. I smelled smoke, he has burned the sacred scrolls of the great elders, taught my children to forget, taught them guilt, taught them fear, taught them to love flesh, gave them war, gave them the "choice" to live or die, taught them that rocks they kicked around on the ground were called diamonds and have value, taught them that women are evil by nature. He polluted our waters, raped and desertified our forests, Pointed all success westward. I gasped for air and still couldn't breathe.

I reached in my pocket and found a letter. I read the letter. He took my crown and my power, he said, but would not destroy me. He wanted me to see the fall of humanity. The stranger gave me two choices. Two things he felt would keep me exiled, He stated that I could be the wind or ink. The letter read: "The wind, snared by skyscrapers, **will no longer be appreciated**, and the soil will be replaced by concrete. Ink too, will lose its effectiveness after I manipulate all reading material to confuse the reader. To my aid will come the television and the radio. The ears and eyes receive information. The mouth is no threat to me. It can only project information and will face great opposition when facing the ears and eyes that I have already infected."

I weep for you my children but cannot cry. It's been seven centuries since I made my choice. I chose ink. I can only hope that the reader and I connect. If that should occur, then my children will someday read and be free. As the author lifts his pen to think, I catch my breath. I **will** rule again…

True Story

I'm very hungry, I have to get something to eat. Where are my keys? There they are, let me lock this door. Wow, it's hot and humid. Lightning stretches across the sky but no rain. As I walk towards my car I fight depression. It seems as though I'm floating. While at the side of my car I notice that my rear driver side tire needs air. I start my car. I need an oil change, I think to myself. A brief moment of fear hits me as I wonder if I locked the door to my apartment. If something happened to my family, I don't know what I'd do. Think I'll get Chinese food. Everything around me slows down so I can catch up. As I order my food, a bead of sweat forms on my brow. A lady walks into the restaurant wearing a Hawaiian print dress; high heels, no stockings, her purse resembling a gym bag hanging on one strap, complexion of a pear, and her hair slightly a mess. The restaurant is on a dark block, and it is too late for her to be out, I think to myself. She greets me and I nod with no expression. I can now feel sweat outline my face and hit the floor. It's so humid tonight. "Excuse me, can you open this?" the woman asks. It's funny because it is just me and her in the restaurant. The way she asked me, you would think she was talking to someone else. Her arm extends and at the end of it I see a bottle of mascara in her little hand. Split between not wanting to be bothered and showing my masculine strength, I take the little bottle. She leaves it to me as if she's done it before. I dry the sweat from my hands and try to grip the bottle. "I can't open it, I'm sorry," I say. This sadly follows my heroic gesture. She smiles and takes back the bottle, probably thinking to herself, "Thanks for nothing weak ass!" I see a bug struggling for life. His wings seem to fail him. His balance is off. Should I kill him to finish his misery? What if he escapes his problem? Another bug with the same problem to his left, what's going on here? Somewhere in between dying bugs and distressed women my food is ready. Thanks! I step past the bugs and out of the corner of my eye I see her looking down with the saddest look on her face. She shows signs of tears to come, as the sky shows signs of rain. On my way to my car, I wonder if I could have helped the damsel in distress or the helpless bugs. I look down and see five crushed rose petals on the ground near my foot. I didn't recall seeing them when I arrived. I quickly look up, to ensure that I was the only one on this empty black street. I drive, finally reaching home. Walking to my door, my echoing footsteps make me feel as though I am the only man on Earth. "Where are my keys?" I whisper to myself. "Ah, there they go. I did lock the door." Damn doors, they're so hard to open when the paint sweats. "Let me lock this door behind me."

CRACK. Lightning rips the sky and, accompanied by thunder, rain finally falls. Just in time.

The Weak Eat The Weak

He knew he was hot, conceit an understatement. Those memories of a pudgy little child were far gone. The mirror smiled back at him. He scratched his brow and chuckled slightly to himself, thinking of all the women who had become victim to him. He wondered if he could get **100** women to give him their love and their body on the first night. A slight glance in the mirror reassured him that he could complete the task. As his first victim undressed, the game had begun.

Tall, short, fat, thin – all shades and sizes came and went. They laughed, they cried, he conquered. After a while he only saw numbers, no faces.

His effortless game soon became a weight. His conscience and ego became a double-edged sword that would soon draw blood. Losing track of numbers and time and noticed **#70** on his list. Her beautiful brown skin, cotton-soft hair, mahogany brown eyes, long legs, and beautiful smile all but blew him away. After their evening together he felt different. He felt like a new man. He soon notices he's stuck on **#70**. He reminds himself to stick to the game plan. Trying to forget her he throws water on his face while looking in the mirror. He notices for the first time in his life he is truly happy.

He thinks he just might love **#70**. One Sunday they are eating in a cafe when his friend walks in. He jumps up fast, seemingly as if the waitress has spilt hot tea in his lap. He has told his friends about the challenge and couldn't let them think that he had failed. I'll be back **#70**. He meets his friend at the waitress desk and pulls him into the restroom. "Hey, what's up?" his friend asks. "Nothing, I was just leaving," he answers.

"OK, Hey! whatever happened to that 100-women challenge?"

"Nothing happened to it, I'm right on schedule," he says.

"How many more do you have left," his friend asks. "Thirty!" he answers, seemingly annoyed.

"I'd like to put a wager on that," his friend urges. His inner beast awakened, he yells, "You're on!" But he secretly vows to himself that after the challenge, he and **#70** would make preparations for marriage.

"Hey man, before I go, I meant to ask you, how do you explain your early departure to all those women?"

"Oh, I tell them that **"all I needed was one day"** and then I thank them," he replies.

"All I needed was one day, thank you," #74. **"All I needed was one day**, thank you" **#88**.

He moves **#70** into his home. Twelve victims left to the end of the game. It would be the end of his selfishness and the beginning of his happiness.

Eleven down, one to go. The night arrives and he is happy to finally end the game. "**All I needed was one day**, thank you" **#100**. He instantly smiles to himself, it is finally over. He rushes home to **#70**, nervously rehearsing his proposal. When he reaches home he finds an empty apartment. There are none of her clothes in sight. It is almost as if she had been a dream. The only thing confirming her existence is a letter on the bed. He takes a deep breath, opens the letter: **"Thank you, but all I needed was one month."**

Goddess

Trying to speak to God about loving my enemy is so hard to do with a knife in your lungs. God asked me, "Do you believe everything you read?"

"Didn't you say 'Love your enemy'?" I asked.

"No, I didn't. Loving your enemy isn't necessary and, to be honest my son, it isn't very smart. I meant for you not to harness any cruel intentions against anyone who hasn't harmed you, your family or your ancestors. You should keep your enemy in sight and be on guard. Stay close enough to see his next move but far enough to fire back and get your family away unharmed. Remember, he's the enemy and should be treated as such.

"Discernment, free will and common sense are gifts that I have given you to navigate life. Don't be a slave to words written on a page by men whose intentions were hidden. The most important gift I have given you is your partner. You are a King, where's your Queen?"

"I didn't know I had one, I replied. "Look in the mirror," God said.

"I don't understand. You mean the woman that looks like me," I asked.

God said, "Exactly! Find your emotions. They will save you and your family. Keep your mind and body your own."

"That's not in the Bible," I said.

"Do you have to read things to believe?" God asked. "Sometimes with a book there is a problem in not knowing the motives behind its creation. Who, what, when, why, and where helps grow ripe fruit. Without these questions answered it challenges any translation, making comprehension impossible. It can reduce righteous teachings into rhetoric. Man-made isn't made by me."

I smiled and said, "There's a big difference between Frankenstein and Dr. Frankenstein. Can I open my eyes now?" I asked.

"Practice patience my son, your basic instructions are almost done. Love isn't for everyone, trust isn't for everyone. These must be earned. All you have is your land and your Queen, for she is your family and future. Your land is your freedom. Land should never be shared; it is as sacred as your mother's womb. No one will ever make any more land. I will never protect anyone who tries to take these things away from you."

"Why do we only have one life, God?" I asked.

"Do not think of it as one life but the first stage," God said. I must ask, who is this 'God' you speak of?"

"That's you," I said.

"Did I tell you my name was God?" God asked. "No," I replied.

"Don't worry about my name; just respect yourself, nature and humanity. Love is an action not just a word. I am and I exist. I don't exist in your comfort level but in truth, time and space.

"Open your eyes my son."

I opened my eyes and saw the world but heard nothing. Suddenly the voice changed. A woman said, "Turn around."

"Why did you change your voice?" I asked.

She said, "Because you believe not what you see. That's why you believe a man could be created first when you see with your own eyes that woman creates life every day.

"I had to communicate in a way that you could understand me," God said.

"You are the first man, my first son. I must now take you to meet your Queen," she said.

"Take what I've taught you and recreate humanity. The first time I tried didn't go well at all. Take more responsibility. You don't have to only look up to see me. I am in all things, and remember, if you fear me, you can't love me."

The Vision

You are the company you keep, you are what you eat, and birds of a feather flock together, as my mother used to boast. I daydream while walking in the park accompanied by my son and two daughters. Every Sunday I take a break from my busy schedule and enjoy time with my children. The park is the perfect place to relax and observe people and nature.

At my birth my great grandmother performed an ancient ritual called "***Fessing***", giving me the power to turn the innocence in my heart into what we like to call "True Vision". This power makes it possible to see people's true feelings and nature. We are able to decode persons and situations in seconds, by traveling through rays of light, folding time onto its side, freezing everything around us and for a split second giving us a better understanding of what we see.

As one gets older, True Vision can simplify more complex personalities and situations by using codes or numbers. But as a child the visions usually occur in the form of pictures or animals in order to simplify their understanding. My grandmother said that when I had a child of my own she would perform the same ritual. She kept her word by passing my power on to my children. The challenge for me was having three children at once. My mother was always there to explain my visions for me, but I was her only child.

My wife had mixed emotions about the ceremony. She expressed her disappointment in not having True Vision. (Unfortunately, it must run in your family and, more importantly, it must be administered at birth.) However, once the ceremony starts, birth is painless. She never complained about that part. I wonder sometimes how my mother taught me to understand my gift, how to harness that power, to control it. Without control, their vision of the past and future can take the seer anywhere. True intentions may sometimes transform those they see physically into what their spirit shows. My daughter Poet saw our new neighbor as a snake, showing his untrustworthy nature. My daughter Jade saw a woman with two heads and a forked tongue, showing her two faces and gossip-filled interest. Sometimes my children get side effects. They can have terrible headaches, bloody noses, bad ear infections and nausea until the vision subsides or the person or situation leaves or changes. True Vision is a great gift with a great burden. I close my eyes and I can hear my mother talking to me. She always knows when I'm troubled. We can't hear when our True Vision is decoding. We only decipher images and actions at that moment. To communicate we read lips. My mother used to say to me **"you are the company you keep, you are what you eat, and birds of a feather flock together"**. Those words always comfort me. She used them so much in my life it's almost as if she was preparing me for something.

Walking with my children in the park I notice people from all walks of life, which for us means a very busy day. My fear grows knowing the dangers that lie with their visions. If all three visions connect even in their young stage, they can see something I can't. How in the world can I explain something I haven't seen? My daughters' perceptions are more powerful than their brother's and they may experience more in-depth visions. It is a good day so far, the weather is beautiful, my children are smiling. I may have overreacted, I think to myself. "Who wants ice cream?" I ask. All three of my children yell "Me"! A ball bounces in front of me; suddenly it stops in midair. I turn to my three children slowly and it is happening. They're all holding hands; this means their visions are linked. Seconds after their vision I see my children puzzled and silent. Trying to stall their question, I give them ice cream.

We sit on the bench and then my junior says, "Daddy, our vision was weird." Afraid of what I might hear, I ask "What was it about?" He says they saw the entire park full of blind people holding each other's hands and leading each other around. "Daddy, how can they lead someone if they cannot see?" Jade asks. They ask me a question I've always had and never could answer myself. In one second they have found the problem with most of the World.

"You are the company you keep, you are what you eat, and birds of a feather flock together." I smile because I knew how my mother answered my questions as a child. I saw a look of satisfaction on their faces. They all say "okay" in unison. My mother knew that my visions were always more advanced than my years. Trying to explain my visions would frustrate her more than teach me. Some people never answer such questions or have enough courage to ask at all. Her vision gave me a saying that explained the behavior of people in a simple way. She knew that questions sometimes take time. She knew that sometimes people answer questions, and sometimes experience does. One day they will use the saying themselves to their children and thank me for it. I will quickly tell them, "thank your grandmother".

Reflection

Through my toes and under my feet the water washed onto shore. I knew before the waters came that they would leave just as fast. Nothing personal, it's just the order of things that come and go. I noticed that the more the water comes on shore, the more land it takes. The sea is never greedy it takes only what it needs.

I knew she would come into my life and shortly thereafter leave just as fast. Those waters tell a tale. The sun sets, distant waters are now silent. I hear nothing, I see only memories. I must burn the picture in the frame I had in my mind. Her touch, her smile were as soothing as watching roses sway from side to side in the meadow; we tried to touch each one, figuring that we could spread our love throughout the world. Then we would lie at the foot of those roses, not harming a single one. Hearts race as we breathe heavily staring into each other's eyes. Our first kiss, should've known it would be our last from that look she gave me. I tried my best to change the subject after that look but it was too late. She said she couldn't love anyone. She said she only had six months to live, due to a rare disease as a child. I have to go, she cried, getting up and running away screaming, "I can't".

She wouldn't take any of my calls or letters. Three months had passed and I had decided I wasn't taking "no" for an answer. When I arrived at her hospital room, no one was there. The room was empty and her flowers had wilted. I thought to myself, "Why would they take her body and leave me wilted flowers?" She passed away and part of me died with her. The part of me that still lives walks these shores looking for answers. Like those waters, I knew before she came she would leave just as fast. It's nothing personal, it's just the order of things that come and go. These waters will always come and go and so will love, I will never forget her.

The Binge...Why?

The story unfolds pieces of us all. Each morning we awaken to an abundance of time and chances all around us. Our stories build a palace just past the horizon. Along the way we recollect stories from our past that become memories. Each decision, each feeling, each lesson, each experience becomes a story. The self-centered, the wicked, the heartbroken, the innocent, the weak and the disenfranchised all play a part.

Do you like Riddles?

What do you get when babies give birth to babies who then transport fear through their umbilical cords that lie uncut? What do you get when truth takes a back seat to opinion? When the murderer holds the gavel? What do you get when you lie in hope while your death dealer bids on a serum that will extend your life until your death? When Men pick Wives based on Body Parts. When two guns, both with one bullet, are placed on either side of your head? One has a normal bullet, one has a natural bullet. You wonder which one will kill you. What do you get when the six-figure executive is a better person than the wage earner? When pain is force-fed to those who have already force-fed drugs to more of those who have pain? What do you get when houses of money stand tall enough to block the sun and you still want more? What do you get when people knowingly remove their teeth exchanging their smiles for dreams? When a world of mirrors is built and people see only themselves? When lions think they are gazelles? When they fight forest fires for days, and cut down brown wood to make green wood so they can burn it anyway to print more? What do you get when a little boy with the magnifying glass grows older and becomes President? When women associate pain with beauty? What do you get when our taste buds send us to early graves? What do you get when water is only an option? When vegetables and fruit are grown under blue light? When the wicked lie still, the innocent toss and turn? What do you get when feelings become revelation? When the spaces between one's ears resembles the space between jail bars? When men and women disgust one another? What do you get when sex becomes purely physical and perversion is released amongst a world that lies perfect in darkness?

When an orgasm is the determining factor in starting a family? What do you get when you talk to children like adults? When technology becomes adverse nature? When people are secretly and unknowingly watching in the dark? What do you get when the masses are blinded by ambition and personal achievement? The sick are given 90 days, the elderly are given cat food, children are given video games, men and women are given divorces? When a country's standard of living isn't the standard of giving? When people of peace try to talk to warmongers? A massacre is expected. So, what do you get when Mother Nature gets tired of pollution? When she gets tired of over-fished seas, and holes dug in her surface and left there? When animals are taken for granted with a false sense of human superiority? When she heightens magma's temperature? When she builds 300 mph winds that create waves that block the sun? When earthquakes split every square mile of land under your feet?

I think you know what you get…

EXTINC

TION

Thank You

Depending on your ability to accept any new ideologies or views that rival your own, a box cutter may be needed in order to Think Outside The Box. (T.O.T.B.) Many years of being told what to think, feel and believe may have caused more anxiety for our soul. Daydreaming and fantasy have helped humanity cope with the pressure of living according to the financial statements of corporations. The war between right and wrong haunts us in our sleep. Our prayers intensify as questions pile up. Humanity loves to be loved. This too may be exposed through glass walls. Why has the mirror taken all of our beauty? Why has love destroyed so many relationships? Is there a difference between happiness and satisfaction? Is there a difference between peace of mind and Heaven? All of these unanswered questions may have led to your hunger. If you were famished, I hope you feel satisfied knowing that you've come to the right place. Please feel free to return anytime you need to nourish your mind, body and soul.

Cessation

Come walk with me…
Let's swim those waters
Feel the wind at our backs
Let the sun bathe us, and land keep us
For we are free, to dream, to hope, to believe,
To be all that they said we couldn't.
Let the clouds envy our heights
And the fish, our depths
Let no one take from you that which they didn't give

www.ingramcontent.com/pod-product-compliance
Lightning Source LLC
Chambersburg PA
CBHW021424070526
44577CB00001B/51